DON'T
THE OF

By

REG FRARY

With illustrations by

ROD

NORHEIMSUND BOOKS AND CARDS
1 Whitney Road,
Burton Latimer,
Kettering
Northamptonshire
NN15 5SL

DON'T BLAME THE ORGANIST was first published by A.R. Mowbray & Co. Ltd in 1963. Republished by Norheimsund Books and Cards in 1993.

Cover illustration by
Caroline Boyes

By the same author

DON'T UPSET THE CHOIR
WHAT ABOUT THE CHOIR, VICAR?
HAVE YOU HEARD OUR CHOIR?

ISBN 0 948852 37 2

Printed by Peter Dawes Printers
6 Canon Street, Kettering, Northamptonshire
Tel: (0536) 85524.

DON'T BLAME THE ORGANIST

The cat gave the unmistakable impression that he was laughing at us

FOREWORD

THE choir sings too loudly, the choir sings too softly, too slowly, too quickly. The choir sings too little, the choir shouldn't sing at all. . . .

As a chorister of many years standing I was conscious of the high esteem in which our choir was held by clergy and congregation alike. I wondered if other choirs enjoyed so much appreciation.

During holidays I have continued my custom of gate-crashing wherever I have found a church with the slightest suspicion of a choir. And I've found out . . .

REG FRARY.

TO ANNABEL

DON'T BLAME THE ORGANIST

HARK! THE GLAD SOUND

A CHRISTMAS spent in a small Dorset town gave me a wonderful opportunity of joining the Parish Church choir in their traditional Christmas Eve carol singing at the local hospital.

This delightfully ramshackle Victorian monstrosity, affectionately known as the slaughterhouse, was held in the very highest esteem by the townsfolk. Like the parish church and the gasworks it was part of their heritage, and they made strenuous efforts to oppose all attempts by the Department of Health and Social Security to close it. They made even more strenuous effort to ensure that none of them, however ill, ever entered the place.

Generally, therefore, a large number of beds remained permanently vacant, but lately business had improved. Outside the hospital the road was very narrow and the Council had embarked on a vast programme of improvements. This had gone on for months, and appeared to consist solely of a large waterlogged hole, carefully surrounded each night by half-a-dozen unlighted oil lamps. Unwary travellers then drove headlong into it, and had only to be trundled a few yards into the hospital.

On this Christmas Eve, as was the cherished custom, the choir arrived at the tradesmen's entrance fully robed and fully half an hour late. We were greeted by the matron who was obviously brimming with the seasonal spirit of goodwill. 'Wipe your feet,' she rasped encouragingly, and placed her ample form solidly in the way until we had done so. We then followed her down a series of arctic passages smelling of disinfectant and onions to our first port of call, a ward full of elderly ladies.

We filed in, smiling and murmuring Merry Christmases to the patients, who greeted us with dignified silence, their dear old faces transformed into masks of maniacal fury. A choirman next to me whispered that this was really quite understandable. To accommodate us a nurse had just turned off the ward television in the most exciting part of the special Christmas Eve gangster film, in which a mob of maladjusted layabouts were beating up a policeman in Big Lou's Pool Room.

Bravely we assembled round a Christmas tree in the middle of the floor, and I noticed we had been joined by two new characters. One was a large yellow cat who gave the unmistakable impression that he was laughing at us, and the other was a middle-aged lady who reminded me strongly of a pencil. I gathered that she was a Miss Selina and was kindly to accompany us on her violin.

The first carol was 'Good King Wenceslas,' and as the choir possessed three tenors who all thought they were indispensable the part of the King was sung in triplicate. This unfortunately rather overawed the page boy, causing him to miss altogether his soprano complaint about the dirty night. However, we all trickled in gradually, and attention was drawn away from the boy by Miss Selina, who was setting everyone's teeth on edge with her unique accompaniment of the famous carol.

We followed with two or three more well-known carols in which to my surprise the Matron joined. She was standing behind me, but I recognized immediately that forceful 'Wipe your feet' roar as it asserted itself, speeded our flagging tempo, and with the utmost ease flattened us a tone per verse.

Finally we came to Miss Selina, who announced coyly that she would now play a 'Christmas piece.'

I am not a competent judge of violin playing, and I don't quite know what she was trying to do, but it was interesting to note that during the performance the oldest patient had to be forcibly restrained from walking out—and the yellow cat rolled all over the floor in a wild ecstasy.

Our reception at the next stop—the men's ward—was far less violent. Here the patients had been able to see the end of the TV gangster film, and when we arrived were peacefully settling down to sleep.

Of course, we soon altered all that when we opened up with 'Silent Night.' Miss Selina's violin just didn't blend with our voices, especially as she was playing 'O Come, all Ye Faithful' for the first few bars. There was a sudden movement right down the ward as patients began to prop themselves up or bury their heads under the bedclothes. We saw no more of the buried ones, but the rest seemed genuinely interested. It was indeed encouraging to overhear a man in a bed near me call out to his neighbour that this looked like being a very funny turn.

The yellow cat now attached himself to me, fondling round my ankles and purring. Perhaps he sensed that I was a cat lover, or perhaps my alto voice intrigued him. Anyway, he still seemed to be laughing. The choir soon got under way with another selection of carols sung in our usual swashbuckling, devil-may-care manner—and with more success this time. The Matron had threatened to take command again, but during the singing of 'The First Noel' had been urgently called down the ward to a very obstreperous patient. He was a well-known music teacher and was threatening to throw a fit and sue the Department of Health and Social Security. . . .

After inflicting ourselves on two more wards we were thanked by the Matron in her most threatening tone. She handed us some curious basin-like cups full of alleged tea, and having disposed of this we were allowed to go.

As we reached the exit there approached us a large genial porter who really radiated the spirit of Christmas goodwill. Beaming all over his face he asked us kindly to stand aside to let the stretcher bearers through. They'd just caught another customer down the hole in the road.

A MINOR PROBLEM

I DISCOVERED the church quite by accident. I was spending a week-end in a famous cathedral city and, having finished my sightseeing earlier than anticipated, I decided to visit a nearby village with which my family once had connections.

It was on one of those delightful country bus routes where the transport company can always get you there but can never seem to arrange the timetable to bring you back. Realizing this too late, I started to return from the village on foot, and on my way stumbled on the church.

It wasn't anywhere in particular, and was hiding behind a row of sinister looking yews. Inside the ancient porch a curly notice clung desperately to a board by one bent tin-tack. 'This church is open daily . . .' it announced, and trailed off into an oblivion of weather-beaten tatters.

A great padlock held the door firmly closed, but this didn't deter me in the least. I knew from experience that in many places it is still a time-honoured custom to welcome the visitor through the most inconspicuous and inaccessible door in the church. After a search, in which I tore my jacket on a bramble bush and turned my ankle on a weed-bedecked gravestone, I discovered a small door behind a flourishing bed of nettles. The door gave easily to my touch, and, following a short, sharp drop I found myself in pitch darkness on a heap of coke in the stoke hole.

As I emerged again, removing coke and a spider from my trouser turn-ups, a youthful voice announced shatteringly,

The most inconspicuous and inaccessible door

'All the runners and betting!' and from behind a vault there appeared a large, round child, carrying a bundle of parish magazines. It stood watching me intently. It wore a colourless boiler suit, and its face was framed in prickly blond hair. Its sex defied identification. It said: 'My father sings in the choir.'

I never know quite what to say to children, but here I was on home ground. 'Oh, good,' I replied encouragingly. 'That's nice, isn't it?'

The large round one thought about this for a moment. 'I don't know,' it answered slowly. 'My father sings with a big, loud voice and they stand him at the end of the row away from the vicar.'

'Oh,' I said, not quite so assuredly. 'I suppose he sings bass then?' Again the child meditated, rubbing its prickly head. 'No, I don't think so,' it decided. 'I think he sings chronic. That's what the vicar says, anyway.'

Mercifully, before I had to think up a rejoinder for this, a burly young man carrying a scythe appeared from behind the chancel. The large round infant's face lighted with pride. 'That's my father,' it announced. 'He sings chronic.'

I immediately established friendly relations with Father, who was most pleased to learn that I was a fellow-chorister. He suggested that he should show me round the church, and on releasing my hand from a vice-like, stable-scented grip, he climbed in through a window and opened the vestry door.

He took me first to see the organ which he said was a wonderful instrument, which hadn't worked for years because the pumping handle was broken and the veteran who used to operate it, dead. 'We use a harmonium,' he explained, indicating a glorious piece of Victoriana perched half on the chancel step and half on a piece of fallen masonry.

The large, round child who was by now standing on its head in the churchwarden's pew, shouted up the church, 'I'm going to be in the choir when I'm five; I shall be out of the way while Mum cooks the Sunday dinner.'

Father glanced admiringly at his offspring. 'The kid'll make a wonderful singer,' he assured me. 'Our family is all the same.' There seemed no answer to this, and we both continued to gaze silently at the child until it lost its balance and fell with a clatter into the aisle. Father then stirred himself from his fond anticipations and said he was sure I would like to see the choir's large music library which had been almost entirely built up in recent years by a generous local benefactor.

We returned to the quaint little vestry. It had so much ivy growing across its latticed windows that everything looked dark green, and we could hardly see where we were going. Father lighted the gas, and dragged back a curtain revealing the music library housed in two large porridge-oats boxes.

I examined a number of well-known anthems and settings and was at once struck by the fact that they all appeared to be brand new and unused. I mentioned this to Father, who gave me a look of amazement, tinged with pity. 'But we don't *do* 'em,' he said incredulously. He pointed to a small, tattered jumble of music copies on top of the piano. 'These are the ones we *do*. Why, we've sung the same anthems at all the big festivals for *years* and *years*. Our congregation likes to know what they're in for. They don't stand for all this messing about with new stuff.'

My guide now led me into the chancel to view the choir stalls, which he said were very interesting. He was right. The book rests and backs of the seats were a glory of amateur carving, carried out by generations of choristers who wished to perpetuate their names in that ancient place. Father showed me his name, cut so deeply that a book rest seemed to be in imminent danger of collapse. 'They do something like this at St. George's Chapel, Windsor,' he informed me—'only *there* the names are on metal plates and are Knights of the Garter or something.'

As we left the church the large, round child was stacking the missionary pamphlets neatly into a heating stove.

'Come on, Fred,' called Father.

At last I knew! 'What a bright little boy,' I enthused. Father regarded me, puzzled.

'Frederica's a girl,' he said.

SACK THE LOT!

THE church choir in which I sang as a guest a few months ago was a downright disgrace. The vicar didn't think so, and the organist didn't think so, but the parochial church council did.

And I had arrived at their ancient village church, somewhere in Norfolk, at a most crucial moment. As I robed for Sunday Matins my uncle, who had introduced me to the church, told me about the awful row at the last P.C.C. meeting.

It was all started by a very respected member of the congregation, who had slept in the front pew for years. It appeared that lately, whenever he opened his eyes, they fell upon the sight of choirboys twisting each other's arms, and the choirmen making eyes at the choirgirls.

He had stood this for a considerable time without complaint, he said, but now felt compelled to bring the matter to the notice of the P.C.C.

The P.C.C., who for the last six meetings had been bored stiff by completely non-productive discussions on the renewing of the church's lethal electricity system and the replacing of the vicar's veteran kitchen range, were only too pleased to welcome a little variety by having a go at the choir. It was always pleasant to have a go at the choir, anyway.

One man, who had been firmly rejected as a chorister owing to the fog-horn quality of his voice, rose to support the front-pew sleeper. Far be it from him, he said, to criticize the choir, but discipline must be maintained. When he was principal bass of the Little Withering Choral Society the discipline was *most* strict. He then recited a whole list of choral societies where the discipline had been most strict, and where, incidentally, he had also been principal bass. Judging by the large number, one gained the impression that he had been handed over from one society to another with the utmost haste until he'd encountered a brick wall in the shape of our unappreciative village choirmaster.

This speaker was now rapidly backed up by the local retired colonel. The colonel, who always made a speech at church council meetings whether he had anything to say or not, and always started off with, 'Of course, in *my* day . . .,' ranted on for a quarter of an hour, finally working himself up to a stirring call to 'sack the lot!'

No one took much notice of him, because he was always sacking some lot or other, but when the village postmistress took the floor there was a sudden respectful attention. It didn't pay to ignore this frail little lady, who by her very calling knew more about everyone's business than they knew themselves. Experience showed that it was far better to humour a character who knew all about you, and who kept the only shop for miles.

She said demurely that the whole thing made her blush with shame. To think that members of the choir above *all* could act in such an abandoned manner. . . . She felt that a sub-committee must be formed immediately to deal with the emergency.

She revelled in sub-committees. Members met almost daily over her counter, between intervals of obtaining the paraffin oil, bacon and family allowances.

The postmistress was followed eagerly by more members, who stumbled incoherently over words which they fondly imagined to be devastating broadsides at the choir. But the vicar, ever faithful to his singers, had managed to delay any definite decision—he was very good at delaying definite decisions—until members of the council had had one more opportunity to observe the choir on Sunday morning.

So now the test was at hand, and the choir filed slowly into church, the organist's plea not to twist each other's arms or make eyes at each other fresh in our ears.

The church was packed. Every single member of the P.C.C. had made a special effort to be there. Indeed, I learned later that one member was so concerned over the shameful slackness of the choir that he had even foregone his customary Sunday trip to the coast in order to keep an eye on them.

The vicar regarded the choir nervously, obviously hoping that on this occasion they would heed his oft-repeated—and ignored—warning about keeping their voices down during the service, particularly in the parts where only he was supposed to be speaking. He need not have worried.

The choir was sphinx-like. The anthem was Elvey's 'I was glad when they said unto me, we will go into the House of the Lord,' and when they came to the passage, 'peace be within thy walls'—the composer repeats the word 'peace' softly, several times in succession—it seemed that the whole congregation were lulled into a false sense of well-being. The P.C.C. members looked particularly shamefaced as they shuffled down the aisle at the conclusion of the service.

In fact, one of the more gullible members, a lady who was now feeling very guilty over the churlish manner in which she had attacked the choir at the meeting, went round to the vestry in order to congratulate the boys on their exemplary behaviour. Most of them had already disappeared, lightheartedly gambolling across the vicar's kitchen garden, but the organist managed to locate two who were locked in a death struggle in the churchyard.

Lightheartedly gambolling across the vicar's kitchen garden

Hastily separating them and wiping away the blood, he presented them to the lady, who beamed on them, shook their filthy hands, and went away with a conscience much eased.

Only the colonel, who hadn't liked the hymns and didn't agree with the sermon, stuck to his guns. As my uncle and I passed within earshot he was declaiming to a rapidly diminishing audience: 'Sack the lot! Why, in *my* day. . . .'

SMELL THE DIFFERENCE

THE receptionist at the hotel where I was staying said that the old parish church had been destroyed by bombing in the war, but they now had a nice new one. She'd never been inside it, 'No time these days, somehow'—but everyone told her it was very nice. She was sure I would find it very nice.

So I set out to look for the very nice new church—and very nearly made a fool of myself. It was only at the bottom of the road, but after half an hour of futile wandering I was on the point of returning to the receptionist to report that I couldn't find it, when I spotted the notice board. I had passed the church about half a dozen times, but had thought it was a biscuit factory, or something to do with the National Coal Board.

There it stood, a large concrete and glass cube, attached at one corner to a smaller concrete and glass cube, and surrounded by a yellow gravel path. And the notice board was no less unique. It was in the shape of a triangle supported on a steel tube and coloured red and white. Notices covered its entire surface. There were large posters announcing bingo sessions, whist drives and dances, and at the narrowest angle of the triangle, tucked away behind a bush, was a shy little reminder that services were held in the church.

I entered the place through the plate-glass doors, and was gaping about me in amazement when I noticed, almost in my pocket, a short, middle-aged woman with blue hair and a jutting chin. She glared at me and demanded: 'Well, what do you think of our church?' What did I think of this adventurous break with tradition, this lightness and airiness? Wasn't I thrilled—absolutely thrilled?

She obviously didn't expect an answer, because, without taking a breath she told me that of course I was. I realized, she said, that the church to-day had no time for backward looking and thinking. It must forge ahead with modern buildings, modern methods. . . .

We then forged ahead up the main aisle, and my self-appointed guide proudly pointed out the glories of the square concrete pillars and the delightfully unadorned roof girders. She insisted on walking behind me and instructing me from under my arm. She wore flat, unpolished brown shoes which were so long that they kept scraping my heels as she drove me round the building from eyesore to eyesore.

We halted before one of the floor-to-ceiling plain glass windows. 'No dim religious light here,' she screeched. 'All pure, honest daylight.' And certainly the windows admitted the maximum amount of light. They were also very useful if you got fed up with the sermon, because they enabled you to amuse yourself unobtrusively watching the people outside fuming in the bus queue or taking the dog for a walk to the local tavern.

The woman was now throwing back her blue head and breathing in ecstatically. I thought for a panic-stricken moment that she was going to faint or throw a fit, but I needn't have worried. She hadn't finished with me yet. Her voice softened, and she almost smiled kindly at me as she asked mysteriously: 'And don't you notice something else different about this church?'

I was in rather a quandary here, because I felt sure that if I did mention some of the things I'd noticed different about the place she'd be quite capable of ejecting me forcibly. So I just stood there, smiling and stammering. 'Well—of course . . .'

Luckily she couldn't stop talking for long, and came to my rescue eagerly. 'No churchy smell!' she enthused. 'No fustiness! Good clean air!' She was quite right, of course. Judging by the good clean smell I should imagine that the person who had recently swabbed the floor had upset a whole bottle of carbolic into the water.

And now just for a moment as we stood there sniffing, I had my first chance to lead the conversation. 'Where does the choir sit?' I asked.

She was still enraptured with the carbolic, and I had caught her off her guard. She became quite annoyed. 'We've put them in the gallery,' she said shortly. 'The Victorians paraded them in the chancel. We've nothing Victorian here.' Then smartly she took control again. 'This way,' she commanded, prodding me into the vestry.

I had the sudden vivid impression that I was entering a large shoe box. At one end a bearded young man was sorting through some music manuscripts. My guide introduced him to me as the organist, and he came forward vaguely and shook hands. Looking through me, he said that he liked to feel that his was the finest choir in the diocese. He waved his arms round the walls, which were peppered with prize certificates, and said I could see for myself. He then treated me to a lecture on church music and explained that all the neighbouring choirs and organists were morons, who degraded themselves by pandering to the unspeakably sentimental tastes of their congregations.

When he eventually dismissed me the woman saw me off down the yellow gravel path. She was telling me proudly that in the morning I should be awakened by the sound of bells, but it would not be produced by the wasteful employ of eight ringers. Here again the church was up to date. They used a stereo tape.

On the Sunday morning I sang in the choir of a nearby church. It was a solid red-brick Victorian effort, filled with painted texts and loaded with plaques. The dim religious light filtered through stained-glass windows depicting saintly gentlemen wearing red and blue nightgowns and dinner-plate halos—memorials to a century of Indian Army colonels and local tradesmen.

An outsized brass lectern eagle presided magnificently at the chancel steps, and, yes, there was just that faint suggestion of a churchy smell. The choir sang a popular and thoroughly hackneyed setting of the *Te Deum*. Even the congregation knew it. I felt at home.

THE CHOIR GOES WEST

I WAS standing behind a piece of scenery, frantically trying to learn two lines written on a tattered envelope which I had carried about for six months. The occasion was a village choir's annual winter show, somewhere in Suffolk.

Being well known as a guest member of the choir whenever I visited a relative in that area, I had been invited to take a small part in the show. So there I stood.

On stage, a group of choristers dressed as cowboys sat round an electric light bulb covered with red paper, which was supposed to resemble a fire, but succeeded in looking like a bulb covered with red paper. The cowboys were all shuddering and clutching weighty blankets about themselves as one announced, 'How cold it is on the prairie to-night!'

The acting was quite good, but was somewhat spoilt because a particularly warm night and a particularly well-stoked boiler, allied to no ventilation whatsoever, had turned the village hall into an oven.

One cowboy, perspiration trickling freely down his face, now stood up and suggested that they should all sing to keep warm. This was greeted by much applause and was also my cue to enter. I was the only alto they had, so they were obliged to get me on to the stage somehow.

I (who feel ridiculous in a check shirt and ten-gallon hat) strode from behind the scenery and announced urgently, 'There's a rider a-comin' up the trail, and he's-a-comin' mighty fast!' This was followed by the sound of two halves of a coconut being clapped slowly together in a manner suggestive of a very old and tired horse just about staggering to a halt. The newcomer was our principal bass, in the guise of the sheriff and the singing group was now complete and rarin' to go.

I can't remember the details of the plot or even why we were all sitting about on the prairie round the electric light bulb, but I think we were supposed to be carving an empire out of the wilderness. Characters in Westerns are always carving empires out of the wilderness, and this is usually done by rustling cattle, holding up the stage-coach, or discreetly blasting half a mountainside on someone's head at Dead Man's Gulch. However, as this was supposed to be a musical Western we remained peacefully singing cowboy songs until the interval.

The audience really entered into the spirit of the thing, and I was interested to note that they seemed to know the ballads far better than the hymns on Sunday. At any rate, they didn't gape in shocked amazement when anyone sang above a whisper.

During the interval, after the stampede for free tea and biscuits had subsided, the Vicar said he was delighted to see so many parishioners enjoying themselves, and hoped that they'd think the choir's efforts were worth a large donation in the plate at the close of the show. As they all knew, the money was to go towards the producing of a new boiler for the hall.

One churchwarden, who by now was almost collapsing with the heat, was heard to suggest that what the hall needed was a refrigerator, but he was always complaining about something and nobody took any notice.

An impossibly ancient lady sitting in the front row then violently demanded of the Vicar when they were going to get some action into the play. In the Westerns they had on the telly, she said, people got shot and strung up all over the place. They didn't keep lazing about on the floor.

The Vicar started to calm her down in the highly successful manner in which he dealt with Church Council members who wanted to get something done. 'Patience, patience,' he crooned, putting his hand on her shoulder. 'All in good time, I am sure.'

A bad man from Arizona way

Luckily for him the curtain rose at that moment and saved him from a rather nasty situation. The ancient lady was not a member of the Church Council, and had no intention of being soothed. But she couldn't complain about lack of action in the second half of our epic.

We were now all in the Red Dog Saloon, where a bad man from Arizona way was trying to terrorize the bartender into giving him free whisky. He waved two plastic guns, and spoke with a strong, homely Suffolk accent, immediately recognizable as belonging to the choirman who was always a beat behind in the hymns and a tone flat in the psalms.

None of the dozen other customers in the saloon dared to come to the aid of the bartender because the badman was completely dressed in black, and in the West this is always a sign of real meanness, and no mercy whatsoever. Whether it be a fine upstanding cowboy, or his poor old widowed mother, the badman shoots on the slightest provocation, or on no provocation at all.

The ancient lady in the front row knew all about this extraordinary type and started to urge the badman to get on with the killing, but at that vital moment, when it looked as though the bartender would be lucky if he only lost a bottle of his best whisky, the swing doors opened and in fell the hero. He shouldn't have *fallen* in, of course, but he was the choir's tenor soloist, who always performed with closed eyes, and had not therefore noticed a choirboy who was crouching behind the doors, holding them up.

From this point the tables were turned, and things went disastrously for the badman. Every time he snarled at the hero, that gentleman struck an attitude and started to sing. This so upset the badman that he could only deflate against the bar and gulp down more free whisky. Certainly the tenor sang convincingly. It was a pity that he was so short and plump, because heroes in Westerns are, of course, always ten feet tall and mighty lean. However, with the aid of confidence and high-heeled boots he managed quite well.

But it was the action that wrung the cheers from the audience. The songs slowed things up. A choirman remarked afterwards that he'd noted the expressions on the faces of the audience while the hero was singing. They were similar to that worn by the Vicar during the performance of a rather long anthem when he was bursting

He pushed the plate closer

to get on with the sermon and aim a broadside at some troublesome members of the congregation.

The Vicar was like that. He kept everyone up to scratch. As I left the hall that night he was standing at the exit, holding the collection-plate a few inches under the nose of a very prominent parishioner. She was an enormously wealthy widow who admitted proudly that since her Children's Church days she had never failed to put her 'Sunday sixpence' in the bag.

'A very good show, don't you think?' the Vicar was saying, 'A *very* good show.' And he pushed the plate closer and fixed her with his beady eye.

RELUCTANT HERO

THE village church organist met me at the station with his car. He had invited me to augment the choir at Evensong, after which, at a special supper, a presentation was to be made to the oldest choir member.

We now drove towards the outskirts of the village to collect this gentleman. The veteran Alfred lived with a married daughter in one of those between-the-wars houses which estate agents amusingly call desirable residences, but which the organist more aptly described as a dump, where you enter by the front door and find yourself in the back garden. On the way I learned about Alfred.

He had sung in the choir for seventy years, had never missed a service or practice, and proudly boasted that he couldn't read a note of music. He'd learned all the tunes by heart as the organist hammered them out every Friday evening, and as the choir had tackled nothing new for the last half-century, he was very proficient. He had never agreed with either the vicar or the organist on anything. Of course, the vicar and the organist had never agreed with each other either, and Alfred had often been hard put to it to disagree with both at the same time. But he had always managed it, and had consequently led a very contented life.

As soon as we arrived at the vestry, two or three choirmen came forward to help Alfred robe. This proved to be rather tricky, because apart from the fact that he wouldn't take off his overcoat, and insisted on wearing a cassock several sizes too small for him, he said he objected strongly to people scratching around him like a lot of old women.

When he had eventually been trussed up like an ill-used parcel, the vicar politely inquired if he was sure he would not like to choose just *one* hymn, as this *was* his special day. Alfred replied that he certainly wouldn't, and appeared to grow really cross. Apparently he had earlier been offered the freedom of the hymn-book and the anthem library for the whole service, but had pointed out that the vicar was paid to choose the music, and choose it he should.

Stainer, Dykes and Barnby had therefore been delved into deeply, in an effort to please, and I for one was delighted. But when Alfred saw the music list his indignation knew no bounds. After all these years, he fumed, that was gratitude for you—putting on stuff he didn't know—ignoring him. . . .

A charming choir-girl who said he was really quite an old dear offered him a throat sweet. Taking a handful Alfred maintained that he didn't agree with such things—smelling the place out. He just had time to put half of them into his mouth before we processed into church.

The nave was packed to the last undusted pew behind the farthest pillar. It would be wrong to say that a sea of faces was turned toward us. This particular church was one of those where they display a large notice outside declaring 'A warm welcome awaits you here,' and when you get inside everyone glares at you as if you are someone from the income tax office. To-night, therefore, even more than normally, the faces were all turned on each other, obviously keeping a sharp look-out for strangers who might be attempting to gate-crash Evensong in order to qualify for the free presentation supper.

No one appeared to notice the choir until the vicar announced the first hymn. Alfred, whom Fate or some other unsportsmanlike character had placed next to me, now whispered in my ear that the whole thing would be ruined by the large bass opposite. He had only been in the choir forty years, and according to Alfred was one of the rising generation who thought themselves too clever to heed what the organist told them.

Despite the bass, the hymn 'Ten thousand times ten thousand,' was sung excellently, and I enjoyed it. I should have enjoyed it even more if Alfred hadn't dropped his large *A. & M.* on my foot at the end of the second verse, and told me I had a very funny voice at the end of the third. The spirit of celebration was in us all. It ran riot. We sang through that service with all the finesse and delicacy of supporters after a rugby international, or a charge of bull-elephants. Stainer, Dykes and Barnby never had it so good.

It seemed that in no time at all we were breathlessly making our way to the village hall for the presentation supper. But as fast as we moved, the congregation had got there first. They were already gathered in smiling groups round large plates of savouries, and were all agreeing that far too much fuss was being made of Alfred. With his voice he should have retired from the choir ages ago. Not that they wanted to be nasty about it, but after all he was *past* it. It was bad enough having a vicar who was past it. No one expected a vicar to know when he'd had enough, but a choirman should have had more sense.

At the right moment the vicar butted in, to make the presentation. He spoke of pillars of the church, and willing horses, and all the joy that Alfred had given with his beautiful bass—or was it tenor?—voice, throughout the

The congregation had got there first

years. Long may he continue to do so, he concluded, and handed Alfred a large inscribed barometer.

Alfred studied it, amid frenzied cheering on all sides. When he could make himself heard, he replied briefly that he already had three barometers—presented when he had retired from the gasworks, the operatic society and the crematorium board, but he supposed he'd be able to stick it on the wall in the scullery, if his daughter would move the mangle out of the way.

Alfred sat down. The guests cheered again and looked round discreetly for some more supper.

SILENCE IS GOLDEN

THE big event of the week-end where I was a guest member of yet another village choir was the annual music festival at the community centre. It was a modest enough affair embracing only a small market town and a cluster of villages, but in the local social calendar it ranked high.

In the church choir section our choir always won the cup. They couldn't help it really. Year after year the chances of the only other entry were zero from the outset owing to the inclusion in their number of a lady who had wild imaginings about the beauty of her voice.

She was also a most generous benefactor of the choir, always eager to pay lavishly for the summer outings and winter dinners. The fact therefore that her alleged voice sounded like a circular saw cutting through a nail carried no weight whatsoever and she was the choir's most popular member.

I travelled from London direct to the community centre and while waiting for our choir to arrive by the local removal van—considered a far more reliable vehicle than the once-a-day bus—I amused myself by listening to the class for solo women's voices. A tall blue-haired lady was on the stage doing her best with something by Vaughan Williams. The only drawback was that she couldn't sing and the noise she made was swamped by the efforts of someone of the Brute Force and Ignorance School who was blasting a trombone in a nearby room.

Understandably I began to lose interest, and was about to move off when I found myself suddenly cornered by one of the many doting mummas in the hall. Dispensing with introductions, she started to bombard me with details of the sensational voice of her daughter Rosie, a large beefy child of about fourteen, who was reclining across three chairs gorging from a pound box of chocolates. Mumma gave me to understand that if the adjudicator was fair—and they were often grossly unfair—Rosie would win her class hands down as she had had a great deal of experience. She had indeed carried out some *very* successful professional engagements.

What her version of these would have been I never knew because at that moment the chocolate consumer was called

Cornered by a doting mumma

to the stage. But I heard later that they were quite authentic. On one occasion Rosie had inflicted herself on the inmates of an old people's home who were too infirm to get away, and on another she had sung 'Because' during the interval at the local cinema. The audience there *could* have escaped of course, but they were all busy buying ice lollies and salted nuts at the time and didn't notice.

Despite such a background the biased adjudicator placed Rosie at the bottom of her class. For a moment Mumma was speechless, and then she started on me again with terrifying vigour. I kept on saying I was sorry, but it didn't help at all. I was never so glad to see our choir tumble into the hall just in time for their appearance on the stage. Squeezing between Mumma and the gas radiator against which I had retreated, I made my cowardly escape.

The test piece for the church choir's class was an unmentionable modern anthem by a composer whose sole talent lay in producing discords. Our choir was good at producing discords too, but I don't think they were the kind the composer had in mind because throughout our performance the adjudicator appeared to be closing his eyes and shuddering. At the end he looked very ill indeed, but he managed to rise to his feet and say we had made a brave try. Words failed him after this, and we all clambered off the stage to the thunderous applause of our supporters who had got a free ride in the removal van.

As usual our choir members were highly satisfied. The adjudicator hadn't said much, but even if he had slated us right and left as some rude men had done in the past, it wouldn't have mattered. So long as the circular saw soprano kept up her efforts in the opposing camp the cup was safe with us, and that meant another huge supper at the vicar's expense after the festival.

We now made our way to the tea bar where an irritable woman stood behind a trestle table pouring out cups of muddy hot water. Her manner, however, in no way dampened the spirits of one of the younger tenors, who was unused to the choir's traditional victories. With a vague idea that he was doing a spot of evangelization he told her that if she wanted to hear some really good singing she should come along to our church on Sunday. This seemed to irritate her even more, and she pushed his muddy hot water at him with such force that half of it slopped in the saucer.

We were trooping out to the removal van when the bomb fell. A member of the rival choir met us in the doorway. He looked pale and bewildered. In the most apologetic tones he told us the awful truth. His choir had won the cup.

'I can't understand it,' he admitted shamefacedly. 'We honestly never meant to upset things. That adjudicator must be mad.'

Our choir simply couldn't grasp the situation. The injustice was too unbelievable. And to add insult to injury something had gone wrong with our rivals' hired bus, and we had to offer them a lift home and the best packing cases in our removal van.

Somehow Rosie's furious mumma also managed to squeeze herself in with Rosie, who almost landed on my lap with another pound of chocolates. Mumma carried on where she had left off earlier. '*Now* can't you see how unjust that adjudicator man is?' she bellowed. 'He ought to be shown up.'

But once again I was saved. The circular saw soprano suddenly appeared on my other side. She'd realized that I was a stranger and the only chorister who hadn't heard from her own lips how good she was. She defeated Rosie's mumma with the sheer speed of her attack, and in one breath had introduced herself and explained just how the Royal Opera had missed the soprano of the century.

Conversation soon turned on this afternoon's victory. Yes, she had to admit she was surprised at that—*reely* surprised. She had appeared with the choir, of course—*moral* support was so important, didn't I think? 'But,' she became very confidential, 'I never told them I had developed a dreadful sore throat last night. I dared not risk *forcing* my voice. I just stood on the platform mouthing the words. I never sang a note.'

UNTO THE THIRD AND FOURTH GENERATION

IN an unfashionable and endearingly British part of London I came across a most interesting parish.

The church had been built to celebrate Queen Victoria's Diamond Jubilee, and the choir and the Church Council had been at loggerheads ever since. The Church Council's jealously guarded grievances were handed down unaltered from one generation to the next, and the present choir did precisely the same things to annoy as their grandfathers did before them. A large proportion of the Church Council had always maintained that the choir should sing more popular music, and a similar proportion never ceased to demand that they should attempt more 'worthwhile' music. A small minority said that they shouldn't attempt anything at all, but they were the people who couldn't sing a note themselves and were rather frustrated.

A half hour before Sunday Evensong was due to start I made my way to the vestry, a delightful place full of wooden forms and lighted by low-powered electric light bulbs in converted gas globes. Its only occupants at that early hour were far too engrossed to notice me. A dreadful little boy with a head like a mop was painstakingly carving his name on the piano, and a refined looking choir-girl was gently telling him that he shouldn't do it. She presently emphasized her words by knocking him from one end of the vestry to the other.

Picking himself up out of a cassock cupboard, the dreadful little boy told her in unprintable language that he would

Carving his name on the piano

inform his father of her extraordinary behaviour and his father, who was a stevedore, would doubtless deal with the matter very drastically. This didn't seem to deter the choir-girl, who advanced on her prey with the obvious intention of repeating the treatment. Then she saw me and asked sweetly if there was anything she could do for me.

I answered respectfully that I'd like to see the organist, and happily at that juncture the gentleman appeared. When he learned that I'd like to sing in the choir he seemed quite pleased in a morbid sort of way. He said that it was an awful job trying to hold a choir together, particularly the boys. 'All morons,' he nodded sadly. 'Not like the boys of our day.' And remembering the budding criminals with whom I trained to sing, I wondered if his memory was playing tricks.

I had no time to meditate on this, however, because my attention was now attracted to a strange procession which had appeared walking across the vestry. It consisted of five large gentlemen, dressed identically in black overcoats and bowler hats, who looked as if they were refugees from a Victorian wedding photo. They were followed by a girl wearing jeans and a pullover which reached below her knees. Without a word they climbed up a ladder and disappeared through the ceiling. 'There they go,' complained the organist bitterly, '—shattering the Sabbath peace!'

It transpired that these were the bell-ringers. What they did in the belfry each Sunday was considered very mysterious and they had nothing to do with anybody. Nevertheless

Refugees from a Victorian wedding photo

they had evoked the organist's undying wrath. They always insisted on pealing the bells right up to the very last minute before the service, and therefore entirely spoilt his pre-service organ recital. For years he had deluded himself into believing that the congregation enjoyed his playing, and for years the bell-ringers had queered his pitch.

Members of the choir were beginning to arrive and an outbreak of mutiny among some of the boys hastily drew the organist away. I was now joined by a choirman who seemed very keen that I should form a favourable impression of the choir. He explained that I should not take too seriously anything I saw or heard in the vestry. It was all the manifestation of a great uneasiness amongst the choir. And it was all the fault of the new vicar. He had swept into the parish like a new and very clumsy broom. With his fanatical smile and barrack square bellow he'd blundered happily from catastrophe to catastrophe. Within the first two months of his ministry he had upset almost everybody. Then, rushing in where angels and six preceding vicars had feared to tread, he'd committed the monumental sin. He'd proposed introducing a new hymn book. The choir were outraged. Indeed, on the Sunday following the announcement two of them had taken immediate steps to discover from the coverless wads of yellowing music in the choir stalls just what hymnal they *had* been using for the last sixty-five years, and the organist broke the habit of a lifetime by arriving at the church for Matins without his *News of the World* to read during the sermon.

The choirman's fascinating story came to an abrupt halt at the entry of the vicar. Having inspected his troops and told us all we looked untidy he straightened the boys' surplices and nearly tripped over his ragged cassock. Then he barked out the vestry prayer and gave the order to advance.

As soon as the service commenced it was obvious his mind was still on the question of the new hymn book. A vicar knows that if he wants to make a change it's always a good idea to get the congregation to imagine that they thought of it first. And this vicar was really working at the idea. Each time he announced a hymn he apologized that the choir didn't have the *better* tune in their books or that the *correct* version of the words was not available to them. Then the sermon gave him his big chance.

But here the seed fell on extremely stony ground. To most of the congregation a hymn book was just a hymn book. They never sang the hymns, and one book was as good as another to hold open at the wrong page. They wondered vaguely why the vicar was getting so hot under the collar. . . .

Of course, the sermon thoroughly upset the choir and after the service they stood about in the churchyard in a state of revolt. Even the bell-ringers processing across the road to the 'Dog and Duck' looked sympathetic. Only one choirman saw the bright side. He sat unperturbed on the church wall and propounded his theory. He had the greatest confidence in the Church Council, he said. They would take years to discuss the vicar's hymn book and by that time, judging by the way the vicar was carrying on, someone high up would have noticed him and given him a job in a cathedral. Then the whole thing could be dropped.

THE OLDER THEY GET. . . .

YOU can generally tell what kind of set-up they have in a country church as soon as you see the churchyard. If the gravestones have been uprooted and stood round the walls like soldiers, and someone has planted a goldfish pond right in the middle of the resulting open space, then you can be pretty certain they've got a progessive vicar and Church Council.

If, on the other hand, the lych-gate falls off its hinges as soon as you try to enter the churchyard and you can't see the path for creeper and bits of broken gravestone it doesn't necessarily mean that things are dead. It's more likely that those in charge are fascinated by rustic charm and don't want to change things or squander any money. You will doubtless find that the vicar is still in the nineteenth century, and indeed has probably been the vicar ever *since* the nineteenth century.

The church I found in the wilds of Hampshire one Sunday morning was definitely of the latter kind. The lych-gate didn't exactly fall off its hinges. I had to lift it off because the latch was firmly padlocked. Fighting my way through the undergrowth I soon discovered that I was not alone. A large number of choirboys were sitting around half hidden among the memorials, listening to a lad with red hair who was speaking from the top of the Manor House family vault. I didn't want to butt in on what was obviously an important meeting, so I asked one of the least dangerous looking choristers on the fringe of the crowd

An important meeting

where I could find the vicar or the organist. He explained politely that he couldn't help me because all the choirboys were on strike. They'd just formed a union and were demanding their rights.

At that moment, however, the organist arrived and broke the strike. He struck me as a man who didn't believe in unions or rights because he achieved his results simply by clouting the red-headed speaker with a manual of organ voluntaries and driving the whole mob into the vestry.

As is my custom I introduced myself, and got invited into the choir for Matins. The organist, a veteran of the old school, explained about the choir. He said the boys weren't a bad lot really. There were a few broken windows from time to time of course, and one of the organ pipes had recently disappeared. 'But it's the *men* who are the trouble here,' he complained. 'They lead the boys *on* so. Never do anything with the boys while they are in the same vestry as the men.'

So the men had now been segregated in the tower room above the vestry, and the boys were almost manageable.

The organist showed me the spiral staircase leading to the tower room. 'Go right up,' he invited. 'Someone will find you some things to wear. I believe the old verger's cassock is still there. No one has worn it since he died, and he was just about your size.'

At the top of the stairs I entered a cell-like cavern full of brown photographs of Victorian vicars and the smell of boot polish. A dozen or so men in stockinged feet were padding round an enormous refectory table on which stood a vase of dead chrysanthemums and a mass of muddy boots. I again introduced myself, and one man who was attempting to clean the boots offered me the only chair in the place. He was most friendly, and before I'd had time to remove some more boots and a pile of dirt from the chair he was well into his story.

Apparently the traditional way for the choir to approach the vestry (and most choirs *are* traditional in their approach despite new vicars who always want to alter everything) was through an alley known as Lovers' Lane, which was always full of mud and broken bottles. It was possible to avoid the broken bottles but not the mud, thus the ceremony of the boot polishing always preceded a service.

Being unacquainted with this particular Lovers' Lane my shoes were reasonably clean and I felt very much out of things. Indeed, I became positively uneasy when I noticed one of the Victorian vicars glaring at me from his brown photograph. He had that Mona Lisa quality about his eyes and wherever I moved he still kept glaring at me. . . .

However, the late verger's cassock fitted me very well and I was as presentable as the rest when the senior choir-boy gave a piercing whistle up the stairs and informed us the 'Old Man' was ready. It was obvious that the vicar was happy in his work. Large and round, he stood amongst us smiling hugely, a delightful ancient cherub. Then at the lift of his finger the talking ceased and the shining boots of the choir plodded sedately from the vestry to the chancel. Our entire way lay across large iron floor grids through which was supposed to issue warm air to heat the church. Something must have gone wrong down below however, because liberal gusts of sulphureous coke fumes were choking everyone for yards around.

But it's possible to get used to anything in time, and it didn't take us long to get into our stride with the first hymn. You could aptly describe the sound as a loud jolly noise, but the tune was based on one of those German chorales which never seem to know when to stop, and I must confess my attention wandered a little. It was finally held by an epitaph on a stone slab at my feet. This was all about a gentleman who had managed to live to 102, and had then been foolish enough to get run over by a steam engine.

The psalms and canticles were sung to chants I'd never heard of, from books that were out of print. Only two men appeared to have copies, and they never opened them.

That, of course, is the advantage of singing the same chants every Sunday for fifty years.

But we kept coming back to the German chorales. The lessons and sermon were short, but the chorales roared on and on, and by the end of the service I had read two dozen more epitaphs.

When we had returned to the tower room some choirmen offered to show me the quick cut through Lovers' Lane, but I was wearing only low shoes so I regretfully declined. As I left the church by the lych-gate the strains of the organ voluntary followed me. I recognized another German chorale.

THE PACK-'EM-IN CHURCH

THEY called it the Pack-'em-in Church. My friend who invited me to sing in the choir explained that a new forward-looking vicar was livening up proceedings, and congregations had grown to phenomenal sizes. It didn't seem to matter whether anyone knew why they were there or what was going on. The idea was simply to 'pack-em-in.'

The church was suburban Victorian and quite unremarkable, but it was impossible to miss it—or rather it was impossible to miss its notice board. This was a huge coloured cinema effort covered with stars and exclamation marks and bearing such thrilling announcements as 'Coming shortly!–Father Bill Bloggs with his electric guitar.'

It was indeed the variety which drew such large congregations. Sunday Evensong had gradually developed into a 'popular' service where all kinds of delightful innovations were introduced so that the young people wouldn't become bored. My friend said that on one occasion recently he had gone home voiceless from an impromptu hymn-singing session in which they had bawled through twenty-four hymns without a stop. On another he had been deafened by a religious jazz get-together which had taken the place of the sermon, and on another, had been completely bewildered by a man who for some reason had talked for two hours on wild life in Outer Mongolia. People turned up in their scores to see what could possibly happen next.

There *was* an orthodox choir, but the only reason that they still functioned was because no one quite knew what to do with them. They were a relic from the bad old days when congregations actually expected to follow a set service. Much to the consternation of the forward-looking vicar the choir continued to attend each Sunday, but he bore it bravely and tried to make out they weren't there.

On the evening of my visit the organist welcomed me and wished me luck. He explained that as far as he knew we should get as far as the *Nunc Dimittis* without things going haywire, but one could never tell. He hoped I'd be able to make out what was happening because he himself often got lost and it was a question of using one's initiative. Apparently the vicar never acquainted him with his plans for a service, but the organist admitted quite freely that this did not offend him in the least. In the revered tradition of organists he never took any notice of what the vicar said anyway. The new vicar merely simplified things for him.

Presently he excused himself, and disappeared into the organ loft to render his brief pre-service recital. This had always been much appreciated by the congregation because it tipped them off that the service was about to start and gave them time to stop gossiping and sort themselves out.

The vicar certainly missed much by spurning the choir. They were the most congenial considerate crowd I had met for a long time. The principal bass in particular was almost embarrassingly solicitous. He asked me if I'd rather sit at the end of a choir stall or at the top. He said that at that end you caught a draught through the memorial window fit to cut your head off, but on the other hand, at the top you were right next to the pre-historic organ blowing motor which made such a noise that you couldn't hear yourself sing. I have a curious aversion to draughts and so elected to cope with the motor.

We marched into church followed by the vicar who beamed at his tightly packed flock, and a jolly young curate who also beamed. He had been specially imported to attract the teenagers, and specialized in playing a jazzed-up version of 'Abide With Me' on a saxophone.

The vicar gained a point over the choir with the very first hymn. Announcing it he enthused, 'Let us sing *energetically* to that joyous new tune we learned at our congregational practice last week. Now! All together!'

No one in the choir felt in the least energetic about that particular joyous tune. They had not been invited to the congregational practice, and they'd never even heard of it. In any case, it wasn't even in their books. Consequently there was a blessed silence from the chancel, except from one very deaf and ancient bass who happily boomed out the tune that *was* in the book.

The vicar conducted at a brisk breakneck tempo with which it was possible to keep pace provided you didn't have to breathe. And judging by the purple faces at the conclusion of the hymn most of the congregation managed it.

During the singing of the psalms the choir had things their own way. Obviously the pointing was a deep mystery to the vicar, and he was sensible enough to let the choir flounder through in the old way rather than attempt the introduction of a new way of floundering. The psalm, however, was a long one, and I suppose he considered we'd had more than our share of the limelight because when the time for the anthem arrived he felt that as the congregation were in such good voice they would like to have a go at another hymn rather than listen to others singing. So as soon as the organist had found the place, and said some things one should never say in the presence of a church organ, we all roared forth again.

Then came the big attraction. The vicar announced that in place of his advertised sermon—it had been advertised in letters of scarlet and midnight blue on the notice board and below the amusements column in the local press—a great friend of his would now give a really intriguing talk, illustrated by colour transparencies, of course, on Old Church Organs. His friend happened to be in the neighbourhood and the opportunity seemed too good to miss. He'd travelled all over the place and knew all about Old Church Organs.

My friend whispered to me that the choir also knew all about Old Church Organs. Their organ was so old it was falling to bits. It had been second-hand when the church was built, and the Church Council hadn't spent a penny on it for donkey's years.

At the bottom of the church a man started setting up a projector, and two others pinned a large white sheet on the chancel screen. Vaguely realizing that the choir were now completely cut off the vicar suggested that they might like to learn something. Would they come down into the nave or go home quietly. We all went home quietly. Only the organist stayed behind. A P.C.C. meeting was in the offing and he wanted to see the Secretary to make sure that the question of the blowing motor was on the agenda. For years he had made sure the question of the blowing motor was on the agenda. . . .

MUD WITH PUG

THE rector was definitely a man's man, a robust outdoor type. His teenage daughter strikingly resembled him. She was called Pug and wore her hair in the style of an ill-used mop, shapeless clothes and what are known as 'sensible' shoes.

I had located the rectory some half a mile from the village church and had called to ask if I might sing in the choir that evening. The rector had readily consented, but had appeared a little disconcerted, I thought, when he learned that I was an alto. 'The *girls* sing that line in our choir,' he said. 'The *men* sing tenor or bass.' However, he invited me to stay for tea and accompany his daughter and himself to church afterwards.

Throughout the meal he told me all about the crafty Church Council who were always holding up his plans for changing the services, the times of the services, and the hymn book. He also spoke with awe about the veteran organist who wouldn't even listen to his plans. He made it clear, however, that everyone concerned was a 'good sort' and that he admired people who stick to their guns. Indeed, he became so enthusiastic about people sticking to their guns that Pug had to warn him that unless he gave over soon we should be late for Evensong

The rector thereupon took off his slippers and put on the largest pair of boots I'd ever seen. He explained that a bus was due in a few minutes, but that we should be walking because generally speaking the bus failed to materialize, and in any case it was more invigorating and interesting to take the short cut across the fields to the church.

Pug had another reason. The original church, she said, was a very fine fourteenth-century building, but during the last century some ham-handed vandal had 'restored' the interior so thoroughly that it was completely ruined. Ever ready to defend the Victorians I mildly suggested that had the ham-handed vandal not restored it, it would probably have fallen down by now anyway. She scorned this unfashionable thought. She considered that the only *bearable* way to view the church nowadays was at a distance from the field behind the graveyard. 'There is a full moon to-night,' she enthused. 'We shall get a *superb* view.'

She now donned a disreputable duffle coat while the rector disappeared into an even more appalling relic. Leaving by the back door the rector led us up the garden path.

I don't know what had happened to the full moon, for apart from being shudderingly cold and windy the night was pitch black. Large pieces of unsuspected meat fat gently stroked my face as we passed under a tree by the gate. Pug said she hung them there for the birds, and she hoped I hadn't knocked any down. Lumbering ahead into a ploughed field the rector continued his monologue about the Church Council and the organist, but I couldn't gather very much of what he bellowed because I couldn't keep up with him for long and the wind was howling in the wrong direction.

At the farther side of the field we came upon a five-barred gate over which the rector and Pug quickly vaulted, and I quickly fell and tore my raincoat. Pug forged ahead, and I made a desperate effort to keep astride of the rector. This was almost impossible as my low shoes had now filled with earth and stones, and were no match for his magnificent clod hoppers, but I felt that as a guest I should at least try to show a little interest in my host's views. 'We have a great musical tradition here,' he was roaring, '—tradition of good robust congregational singing. Organist pulls out all the stops and everybody else throws in all they've got and tries to drown him. Sort of friendly competition. Works wonders with the hymns and gets over the awkward bits in the psalms.'

He ceased for a moment to grab unsuccessfully at my arm as I tripped over a tree root and fell down an unsuspected bank. As I picked myself up Pug reappeared and told me we had now reached the local river. This was an evil looking mess bounded on either side by dead trees which crouched against the skyline like monsters from an Edgar Allan Poe nightmare. Pug said this was a most beautiful spot to spend a long summer evening. . . .

The rector joined me again, and started to explain his plans for getting round the organist's unreasonable objections to changing the hymn book and cutting out the 'Amens' at the end of hymns. But by this time I was so dispirited that I couldn't even trouble to stick to my guns and declare myself all for the organist.

'Here we are,' bawled Pug, from nearby, and I saw that she was untying a half waterlogged wreck of a rowing boat. She splashed into it followed by the rector who seized two broken oars. 'Don't sit on the back seat,' she advised me jovially. 'It's full of the jolly old woodworm.' There was no other seat available so I lowered myself cosily to the bottom of the boat in what she would have doubtlessly called the jolly old moisture.

Cosily seated on the bottom of the boat

We floundered to a halt in the mud on the opposite bank and started to climb one of those banks which amateurs can only negotiate on their hands and knees. As I crawled by his side the rector said that he had at last persuaded the organist to use a new tune for 'Fight the Good Fight' and I should have the pleasure of hearing it to-night. 'It's a step in the right direction,' he gloated, as I slipped backwards down the bank.

Some minutes later as we crossed the last field of our short cut, Pug's voice sung out ahead of us. 'Well, what do you think of that!' She was, I suppose, pointing to the church, but I couldn't see a thing. I didn't even see the half-filled swill bucket which someone had thoughtfully left in the middle of the path. . . .

And then, unbelievably, I stood in the vestry, a muddy disgrace to all altos. Pug's sensible shoes and the rector's brutish boots showed not the slightest fleck of dirt. There is something in knowing every inch of your countryside.

The organist regarded me as he must have often regarded the worst juvenile delinquents in his choir. 'There's some water and a broom in the porch. They might help,' he said doubtfully.

As I crept from his presence trying to persuade myself that I should soon wake up, I heard him apologizing to the rector '—so sorry about the new tune for to-night. I've left the copies at home. Can't think how I came to do it.'

Somehow, deep down, I felt cheered.

DO YOU QUALIFY?

DAUGHTER churches are often very superior to parish churches. Invariably they attract the best preachers. They also attract the people who consider themselves the best choristers.

The choirs of daughter churches get invited to sing at cathedrals, and are always winning cups at music festivals, but among parish church choirs you will find many a cheerful shambles. They never get invited to sing anywhere, are incapable of winning anything, and can sing much louder than three or four daughter church choirs put together.

When I told a relative with whom I was staying in rural Somerset that I should like to sing Evensong in the choir of a certain nearby church he warned me off immediately. 'Don't go there,' he advised. 'You wouldn't get into *that* choir anyway. You go down to the Parish Church. They're far easier there and more up your street.'

I thanked him for being so helpful, but was naturally curious to learn more about the unapproachable church. Apparently it was a very exclusive place and ranked socially with the local golf club. In fact, it was an unwritten law that you should be a member of the golf club before you joined the church.

From time to time some rude pushing person tried to gate-crash without the backing of the club, but they were always expertly put in their place. They were warmly welcomed and someone would immediately fix them up with the job of stoking the boiler, cleaning the inaccessible clerestory windows or polishing about half a ton of brass ornaments. This got rid of them in no time at all, and they soon found their proper level at the Parish Church. This was a venerable ruin full of the most awful people who couldn't tell one end of a golf club from the other and boasting the largest, most unmanageable apology for a choir for miles.

After a few moments' searching questioning the vicar directed me unerringly to the Parish Church. I went directly to the choir vestry, knowing from experience that if you enter by the main door and try to explain to the churchwarden that you want to join the choir, he either looks at you as if you are mad or pushes some books into your hand and says you can sit anywhere.

I also knew from experience that the choir vestry door is always the one round the back, half hidden behind a mountain of coke and dustbins full of dead flowers. So I entered the place with perfect confidence, and was soon happily in the middle of fifty members of the choir who were all trying to robe within ten square feet.

The organist declared that he was delighted to see me, particularly as I was an alto, because thirty of the gentlemen present were basses and things sometimes got a bit top-heavy. . . .

In the chancel there were three rows of choir stalls on either side, and the curate waited politely while we all arranged ourselves in each other's elbow-room. When we eventually attacked the first hymn I didn't seem to have a hymn book, but a number of others didn't either. There was in consequence much shuffling of books and I almost got one by the end of the third verse. Someone did in fact

Arranging ourselves in each other's elbow-room

toss me one but someone else immediately grabbed it away again. By the time we reached the last verse I had settled down to share a book with my neighbour. He was a very short gentleman who appeared to be suffering from a frightful cold—or perhaps he normally sang like that. Anyway the book was half obliterated by a large red handkerchief which trailed from inside his sleeve and allowed me to see only the hymn which we weren't singing on the opposite page.

No one sat below me, so later in the service I edged to the end of the stall in order to examine a pile of rubbish which I thought might contain a hymn book. It was then that I noticed on the floor what appeared to be a large moth-eaten hearth rug. When, however, it began to wag its tail furiously I realized that it was some sort of a dog. He was a most friendly freak and, I learned later, was the bosom pal of the bachelor curate. Unlike so many clergymen, the curate apparently didn't think it sinful and didn't verge on apoplexy every time an animal looked inside a church. The hearth rug certainly didn't look very sinful. He was most intelligent too. He remained bravely at his post during our rendering of the psalms and hymns, but when we came to the anthem he quietly slunk out with his tail between his legs. When we reached the sermon he returned and dutifully fell asleep.

I think the curate was making use of a sermon he had used that morning at the daughter church, because he seemed to be tying up good churchmanship with a game of golf. And from the expressions on the faces of the congregation, who were still conscious, it was obvious that no one had the faintest idea of what he was driving at.

Interest quickly revived at the end of the sermon. The Sunday was within the octave of one of those obscure Saint's days about which only the vicar has ever heard, and we had a procession.

It was the familiar fiasco, dear to the hearts of so many choristers. The boys and girls huddle together and shuffle down the aisle in one glorious discordant mass, followed by the men who straggle, dignified, at a distance, as if to emphasize that they have no connection whatsoever with the firm in front. And at the rear, looking rather embarrassed and singing rather flat, comes the parson.

This particular procession was well on form, and left the congregation wide awake and cheerful. They flowed out of church talking across each other at a tremendous pace and broke up into several animated discussion groups all over the churchyard and the main road. Those on the main road (a courtesy title for the cart track which the Parish Council were always about to 'do up') were soon obliged to move however. A long sleek cortège of expensive black cars purred slowly past. A man told me it contained the entire congregation of the daughter church on their way home to the fashionable outskirts. The whole thing was most dignified. It was perhaps a little marred by one of the Parish churchwardens who drove out of a side road in his veteran paraffin oil delivery van. It got caught up in the middle of the cortège and promptly broke down in a cloud of blue smoke.

It's quite true. Some people are only *fit* for the Parish Church!